101 CUPCAKE, COOKIE & BROWNIE Recipes

Pistachio Thumbprints, page 43

Breezy Kite Cupcakes, page 15

The Best Blondies, page 85

Gooseberry Patch
2500 Farmers Dr., #110
Columbus, OH 43235

www.gooseberrypatch.com
1·800·854·6673

Copyright 2010, Gooseberry Patch 978-1-936283-10-1
First Printing, October, 2010

Gooseberry Patch *cookbooks*

Since 1992, we've been publishing our own country cookbooks for every kitchen and for every meal of the day! Each title has hundreds of budget-friendly recipes, using ingredients you already have on hand in your pantry.

In addition, you'll find helpful tips and ideas on every page, along with our hand-drawn artwork and plenty of personality. Their lay-flat binding makes them so easy to use...they're sure to become a fast favorite in your kitchen.

Triple-Layered Brownies, page 65

Tiny Turtle Cupcakes, page 29

Call us toll-free at
1•800•854•6673
and we'd be delighted to tell you all about our newest titles!

Shop with us online anytime at
www.gooseberrypatch.com

Send us your favorite recipe!

and the memory that makes it special for you!* If we select your recipe for a brand-new **Gooseberry Patch** cookbook, your name will appear right along with it...and you'll receive a FREE copy of the book!

Submit your recipe on our website at
www.gooseberrypatch.com

Or mail to:

Gooseberry Patch • Attn: Cookbook Dept.
2500 Farmers Dr., #110 • Columbus, OH 43235

*Please include the number of servings and all other necessary information!

Have a taste for more?

Visit **www.gooseberrypatch.com** to join our **Circle of Friends**!

- Free recipes, tips and ideas plus a complete cookbook index
- Get special email offers and our monthly E-letter delivered to your inbox
- Find local stores with **Gooseberry Patch** cookbooks, calendars and organizers

Be Mine Cherry Brownies, page 96

Dedication

For everyone who
always saves room
for dessert!

Appreciation

A sweet thanks to
the bakers who shared
your very best treats!

Molasses Crinkles, page 64

Key Lime Cupcakes, page 11

Gail's Pumpkin Bars, page 80

Macadamia & Chocolate Chip Cookies, page 55

CONTENTS

Chocolate–Orange Snowballs, page 61

Swirled Peanut Butter Cheesecake Bars, page 78

Easiest Boston Cream Cupcakes, page 23

Baking TIPS

★ Oven temperatures can vary, so test for doneness after the minimum baking time.

★ Bake up the best texture for brownies and bars...use a wooden spoon to mix in dry ingredients just until moistened.

★ For evenly baked and uniform cupcakes, fill liners about 2/3 full, using an ice cream scoop or measuring cup.

★ Before adding the batter for bar cookies or brownies, mold aluminum foil over the bottom of the baking pan, then pop the pre-formed foil inside.

★ Turn any cupcake recipe into minis...just decrease the baking time by 5 to 7 minutes.

★ If baked cookies are difficult to remove from the baking sheet, reheat the sheet in the oven for one minute, then remove.

★ Keep cookie dough from spreading by cooling baking sheets between batches.

★ Make sure goodies are completely cooled before decorating. Gently brush off any crumbs with a pastry brush or your fingers.

★ Cut brownies and bars smoothly and easily! First, place the pan in the freezer for several minutes. For each cut, dip a plastic knife in hot water, wipe it dry, and move it across the pan in an up-and-down sawing motion.

Orange Puff Cupcakes

1/3 c. margarine
1 c. sugar
2 eggs, beaten
1-3/4 c. all-purpose flour
1 T. baking powder
1/2 c. frozen orange juice
  concentrate, thawed
Optional: zest of 1 orange
Garnish: white frosting, orange
  zest strips

Beat together margarine and sugar in a bowl; add eggs. Combine flour and baking powder; add alternately with orange juice to margarine mixture. Stir in zest, if using. Fill paper-lined muffin cups 2/3 full. Bake at 375 degrees for 15 minutes. Let cool. Spread with frosting and garnish with orange zest strips, if desired. Makes one dozen.

7

Heather Roberts
Quebec, Canada

This is an old-fashioned recipe handed down from my grandmother. The ladies at our annual church social recommend this recipe for our bake sale and tea table.

Cream Cheese-Filled Cupcakes

18-1/4 oz. pkg. German chocolate
   cake mix
1 c. mini semi-sweet chocolate
   chips
1/3 c. sugar
1 egg, beaten
8-oz. pkg. cream cheese, softened

Prepare cake mix according to package directions. Fill paper-lined muffin cups 1/2 full. Combine remaining ingredients; drop by teaspoonfuls onto batter. Bake at 350 degrees for 20 to 25 minutes. Cool completely. Makes about 2 dozen.

Melissa Mishler
Columbia City, IN
These are so delicious, you might want to make a double batch!

Grandma's Banana Cupcakes

Kelly Marcum
Rock Falls, IL

My grandma made these often...so yummy! To make sour milk, stir one teaspoon of white vinegar into one cup of milk and let stand for 5 minutes.

1/2 c. butter, softened
1-3/4 c. sugar
2 eggs, beaten
2 c. all-purpose flour
1 t. baking soda
1 t. baking powder
1 c. sour milk
2 bananas, mashed
1 t. vanilla extract
1/2 c. chopped pecans
Garnish: Cream Cheese Frosting
   (found on page 33),
   banana slices
Optional: caramel sauce

Blend butter for 5 minutes, using an electric mixer on medium speed. Slowly add sugar; beat in eggs. Combine flour, baking soda and baking powder; add to butter mixture alternately with milk. Stir in bananas, vanilla and pecans. Fill paper-lined muffin cups 1/2 full. Bake at 350 degrees for 18 to 25 minutes, until a toothpick inserted in the center comes out clean. Allow to cool; frost with Cream Cheese Frosting and drizzle with caramel sauce, if using. Top with banana slices. Keep refrigerated. Makes 1-1/2 to 2 dozen.

2-Kiss Cupcakes

3/4 c. butter, softened
1-2/3 c. sugar
3 eggs, beaten
1-1/2 t. vanilla extract
2 c. all-purpose flour
2/3 c. baking cocoa
1-1/4 t. baking soda
1/4 t. baking powder
1 t. salt
1-1/3 c. water
60 milk chocolate drops, divided

Beat butter, sugar, eggs and vanilla; set aside. Combine flour, cocoa, baking soda, baking powder and salt; add alternately with water to butter mixture. Fill paper-lined muffin cups half full. Place a chocolate drop in center of each. Bake at 350 degrees for 20 minutes. Let cool. Frost with Chocolate Frosting. Top each with a chocolate drop. Makes 2-1/2 dozen.

Chocolate Frosting:

1/4 c. margarine, melted
1/2 c. baking cocoa
1/3 c. milk
1 t. vanilla extract
3-1/2 c. powdered sugar

Combine all ingredients; beat until smooth.

Athena Colegrove
Big Springs, TX

Bake these for your family and you'll be guaranteed not just kisses, but several hugs, too!

Key Lime Cupcakes

16-oz. pkg. angel food cake mix
3/4 c. lemon-lime soda
1/2 c. plus 1 T. key lime juice, divided
14-oz. can sweetened condensed milk
1 t. lime zest
8-oz. container frozen whipped topping, thawed
Garnish: sweetened flaked coconut

In a large bowl, combine dry cake mix, soda and 1/4 cup key lime juice. Spray muffin cups with non-stick vegetable spray. Fill muffin cups 2/3 full. Bake at 350 degrees for 12 minutes, or until a toothpick tests clean. Cool completely. Use a toothpick to poke several holes almost to the bottom of each cupcake; don't poke through bottoms. Mix together remaining lime juice, sweetened condensed milk and lime zest. Measure out 1/3 cup lime mixture; pour over all the cupcake tops. Stir whipped topping into the remaining lime mixture; chill for one hour. Frost cupcakes with whipped topping mixture. Garnish with coconut. Refrigerate until serving time. Makes 2 dozen.

Lena Smith
Pickerington, OH
I spent the summer trying different-flavored cupcakes. I made these for our church's bake-off and won Honorable Mention!

Pineapple Upside-Down Cupcakes

20-oz. can pineapple chunks,
   drained and 1/2 c. juice reserved
1/3 c. brown sugar, packed
1/3 c. butter, melted
1 c. all-purpose flour
3/4 c. sugar
1/2 t. baking powder
1/4 c. butter, softened
1 egg, beaten
Garnish: maraschino cherries

Pat pineapple dry with paper towels. In a bowl, combine brown sugar and melted butter; divide evenly into 12 greased muffin cups. Arrange pineapple chunks over brown sugar mixture. In a bowl, combine flour, sugar and baking powder. Mix in softened butter and reserved pineapple juice; beat for 2 minutes. Beat in egg. Spoon batter over pineapple, filling each cup 3/4 full. Bake at 350 degrees for 30 minutes, or until a toothpick tests clean. Cool in pan for 5 minutes. Place a wire rack on top of muffin tin and invert cupcakes onto rack so pineapple is on top. Cool completely and top each with a cherry. Makes one dozen.

Sharon Tillman
Hampton, VA

When I was little, every spring my Grandma Bernadean would invite me for a tea party with lemonade and these cupcakes!

Whoopie Cupcakes

1-1/2 c. all-purpose flour
1 c. sugar
1 t. baking soda
1 t. salt
1/3 c. plus 1 T. baking cocoa
3 T. shortening
4 t. vinegar
1 c. milk
1 t. vanilla extract
Garnish: powdered sugar

Combine flour, sugar, baking soda, salt and cocoa. Add shortening, vinegar, milk and vanilla. Beat for 2 minutes. Fill greased muffin cups 2/3 full. Bake at 350 degrees for 20 to 25 minutes. Cool. Cut off tops in an inverted cone shape so it narrows toward the center of the cakes. Fill cupcakes with filling and replace tops; sprinkle with powdered sugar. Makes one dozen.

Filling:

3/4 c. margarine
3/4 c. shortening
1-1/2 c. sugar
4-1/2 t. all-purpose flour
1/8 t. salt
3/4 c. milk, room temperature
1 T. vanilla extract

Beat all ingredients for 8 minutes with an electric mixer, or until fluffy.

13

Janie Corliss
Front Royal, VA
I began making these cupcakes when my sons were babies. They're so much easier to make than whoopie pies and taste just as good!

Special Mocha Cupcakes

1-1/2 c. all-purpose flour
1 c. sugar
1/3 c. baking cocoa
1 t. baking soda
1/2 t. salt
2 eggs, beaten
1/2 c. brewed coffee, chilled
1/2 c. oil
1 T. vinegar
1 T. vanilla extract

Combine flour, sugar, cocoa, baking soda and salt; set aside. Combine remaining ingredients; add to flour mixture and stir well. Fill paper-lined muffin cups 2/3 full. Bake at 350 degrees for 20 to 25 minutes. Cool in tin on wire rack for 10 minutes. Remove from tin; cool completely. Frost with Mocha Frosting. Makes one dozen.

Mocha Frosting:

3 T. semi-sweet chocolate chips, melted
3 T. milk chocolate chips, melted
1/3 c. butter, softened
2 c. powdered sugar
1 to 2 T. brewed coffee, chilled

Combine chocolate and butter; gradually beat in powdered sugar. Stir in coffee until smooth.

Barbara Humiston
Tampa, FL

Invite your best girlfriend over for conversation, a mug of coffee and a cupcake...or two!

Breezy Kite Cupcakes

18-1/4 oz. pkg. chocolate
  cake mix
1-1/2 c. candy-coated chocolate
  mini-baking bits, divided
24 graham cracker squares
16-oz. container white frosting,
  divided
assorted food colorings

Prepare cake mix according to
package instructions. Fill paper-lined
muffin cups 2/3 full; sprinkle each
with one teaspoon baking bits.
Bake at 350 degrees for 20 to
25 minutes; cool completely on
wire racks. Using a serrated knife,
gently cut graham cracker squares
into kite shapes; set aside. Tint half
the frosting blue; tint remaining
frosting desired kite colors. Frost
cupcakes with blue frosting; frost
graham kites with remaining frostings
as desired. Tilt cracker slightly and
arrange on cupcake top. Add a string
tail of mini-baking bits. Makes
2 dozen.

15

Penny Sherman
Cumming, GA
On a rainy day, spirits
are bound to lift when you
serve these pretty cakes!

Chocolate & Marshmallow Cupcakes

8-oz. pkg. unsweetened dark
   baking chocolate, chopped
1 c. butter, softened
4 eggs
1 c. sugar
3/4 c. all-purpose flour
1 t. salt
1/2 c. mini semi-sweet chocolate
   chips
Garnish: 1/2 c. mini marshmallows

Place chocolate and butter together in a microwave-safe bowl; microwave on high setting just until melted. Cool slightly, just until warm. Blend together eggs and sugar until light and foamy. Add flour and salt; mix well. Pour in chocolate mixture; blend until smooth. Fill paper-lined muffin cups 2/3 full. Sprinkle one teaspoon chocolate chips over each cupcake. Bake at 350 degrees for 15 minutes, until a toothpick tests clean. Remove from oven; arrange several marshmallows on top of each cupcake. Broil just until marshmallows turn golden. Remove from oven and let stand 5 minutes to cool slightly. Makes one dozen.

Kathy Grashoff
Fort Wayne, IN

Drizzle with chocolate
or caramel sauce for a
divine delight!

Bears at the Beach

Dolores Adamo
Wallingford, CT

A cute dessert for summer
picnics...so sweet!

17

18-1/4 oz. pkg. favorite cake mix
16-oz. container white frosting
blue and yellow food coloring
24 bear-shaped graham crackers
Garnish: blue and yellow sugar
    sprinkles
24 peach ring jelly candies
6.6-oz. pkg. fruit-flavored snack
    rolls, cut into 24 2-inch
    pieces
Optional: paper parasols

Prepare cake mix and bake cupcakes
according to package directions; let
cool. Tint half the frosting with
blue food coloring and frost half
the cupcakes. Tint the remaining
frosting with yellow food coloring
and frost the remaining cupcakes.
Sprinkle blue cupcakes with blue
sprinkles and yellow cupcakes with
yellow sprinkles. Lay a piece of snack
roll onto each yellow cupcake and
attach a graham cracker with a dot of
icing. Insert a graham cracker
through the center of each jelly candy
and place on blue cupcakes. Insert
paper parasols, if desired. Makes
2 dozen.

Cheery Cherry Cupcakes

18-1/4 oz. pkg. chocolate cake mix
1-1/3 c. water
1/2 c. oil
3 eggs, beaten
21-oz. can cherry pie filling,
    divided
16-oz. container vanilla frosting

In a bowl, combine dry cake mix, water, oil and eggs. Spoon batter by 1/4 cupfuls into paper-lined muffin cups. Spoon a rounded teaspoon of pie filling onto the center of each cupcake. Bake at 350 degrees for 20 to 25 minutes, until a toothpick inserted on an angle toward the center tests clean. Cool completely in tins on wire racks. Frost cupcakes with vanilla frosting; top each with one cherry from pie filling. Makes 2 dozen.

Tina Dillon
Parma, OH

Whenever his birthday rolls around, my husband Terry starts dropping not-so-subtle hints about these sweet treats!

Taffy Apple Cupcakes

18-1/4 oz. pkg. carrot cake mix
1 c. Granny Smith apples, cored, peeled and finely chopped
1/2 t. cinnamon
20 caramels, unwrapped
1/4 c. milk
1 c. pecans or walnuts, finely chopped
12 wooden craft sticks

Prepare cake mix according to package instructions; stir in apples and cinnamon. Fill paper-lined jumbo muffin cups 2/3 full. Bake at 350 degrees for 20 to 25 minutes, until a toothpick inserted near center tests clean. Combine caramels and milk in a small saucepan over low heat; stir until melted and smooth. Drizzle caramel over cooled cupcakes; sprinkle nuts over top. Insert a craft stick into center of each cupcake. Makes one dozen.

Angie Biggins
Lyons, IL

What fun...a gooey caramel-topped cupcake on a stick!

19

Cookie Dough Cupcakes

18-1/4 oz. pkg. yellow cake mix
1 c. milk
3 eggs, beaten
1/2 c. butter, melted and cooled
   slightly
1 t. vanilla extract
16-1/2 oz. tube refrigerated
   chocolate chip cookie dough
16-oz. container chocolate frosting
Garnish: 12 chocolate chip
   cookies, halved

In a bowl, combine dry cake mix, milk, eggs, butter and vanilla; beat for 2 minutes. Fill paper-lined muffin cups 1/3 full. Roll tablespoonfuls of cookie dough into balls. Place a ball into center of each cupcake. Top with remaining batter. Bake at 350 degrees for 15 to 20 minutes, until a toothpick tests clean. Cool in tin on wire racks 10 minutes. Remove from pan; cool completely. Frost with chocolate frosting. Garnish with cookie halves. Makes 2 dozen.

JoAnn
Put the kids to work rolling the cookie dough into balls...and watch so they don't gobble up the cookies!

Hot Fudge Sundae Cupcakes

18-1/4 oz. pkg. devil's food
   cake mix
24 sugar cones
1-1/2 qt. vanilla ice cream
12-oz. jar hot fudge sauce
Garnish: whipped cream,
   peanuts, maraschino cherries

Prepare cake mix according to package directions. Fill paper-lined muffin cups 2/3 full. Bake at 350 degrees for 15 to 20 minutes. Cool completely on wire racks. For each cupcake, top with a scoop of ice cream, drizzle with hot fudge sauce and top with whipped cream. Place the cone into the whipped cream and sprinkle with peanuts and a cherry. Serve immediately. Makes 2 dozen.

21

Jennifer Licon-Conner
Gooseberry Patch

An impressive-looking
dessert that comes together
in a snap!

Almond Petit-Fours

18-1/4 oz. pkg. yellow cake mix
1/2 t. almond extract
3 c. sliced almonds
Garnish: candy-coated almonds

In a bowl, prepare cake mix according to package directions, adding almond extract into the batter. Fill paper-lined mini muffin cups 2/3 full. Bake at 350 degrees for 15 to 17 minutes; cool completely on wire racks. Spread Almond Frosting on half the cupcakes; these will be the bottom-layer cupcakes. Remove the liners from the remaining cupcakes and place them upside-down on top of the bottom-layer cupcakes. Frost the top-layer cupcakes on all sides. Coat cupcake sides with sliced almonds. Arrange candy-coated almonds on top. Makes about 3 dozen.

Almond Frosting:

3 c. powdered sugar
2 t. almond extract
3 T. hot water

In a bowl, combine all ingredients. Beat to desired consistency, adding more water or sugar as needed.

Jill Valentine
Jackson, TN

The trick to this elegant dessert is stacking mini cupcakes. Tint the frosting with food coloring or garnish with sprinkles for variety.

Easiest Boston Cream Cupcakes

18-1/4 oz. pkg. yellow cake mix
3.4-oz. pkg. instant vanilla
   pudding mix
1 c. cold milk
1-1/2 c. frozen whipped topping,
   thawed and divided
4 1-oz. sqs. semi-sweet baking
   chocolate

Prepare cake mix according to package directions. Fill greased muffin cups 2/3 full and bake at 350 degrees for 15 to 20 minutes. Cool completely. Whisk pudding mix and milk for 2 minutes; let stand 5 minutes. Use a serrated knife to cut off the top of each cupcake; set tops aside. Stir 1/2 cup whipped topping into pudding. Spoon one tablespoon onto each cupcake; replace cupcake tops. In a microwave-safe bowl, combine remaining whipped topping and chocolate. Microwave for one minute; stir and microwave an additional 30 seconds. Stir until chocolate is melted; let stand 15 minutes. Frost cupcakes with chocolate mixture. Makes 2 dozen.

23

Robin Hill
Rochester, NY
Our family is known to
enjoy these cupcakes as an
extra-special breakfast!

Double Maple Cupcakes

1/2 c. sugar
1/3 c. plus 2 T. butter, softened
  and divided
1-1/2 t. vanilla extract, divided
1-1/2 t. maple flavoring, divided
2 eggs, beaten
1-1/4 c. all-purpose flour
1-1/4 t. baking powder
1/4 t. plus 1/8 t. salt, divided
1/4 c. milk
1/4 c. plus 3 T. maple syrup,
  divided
1-3/4 c. powdered sugar

Blend sugar, 1/3 cup butter, one teaspoon vanilla and one teaspoon maple flavoring. Beat in eggs. In another bowl, mix flour, baking powder and 1/4 teaspoon salt. In a third bowl, blend milk and 1/4 cup syrup. Add flour mixture and syrup mixture alternately into sugar mixture. Divide batter among 12 paper-lined muffin cups. Bake at 350 degrees for 20 to 25 minutes. Cool in tin 10 minutes; cool completely on wire racks. For the frosting, combine remaining 3 tablespoons syrup, 2 tablespoons butter, 1/2 teaspoon vanilla, 1/2 teaspoon maple flavoring and 1/8 teaspoon salt until fluffy. Gradually blend in powdered sugar. Frost cupcakes. Makes one dozen.

Gail Prather
Hastings, NE
I love using the fresh maple syrup I get at our local farmers' market for these cupcakes...it gives them such a nice flavor.

Chocolate Zucchini Cupcakes

Michelle Rooney
Sunbury, OH
So moist and delicious...no one will guess the secret ingredient is zucchini!

2 c. zucchini, shredded
3 eggs, beaten
2 c. sugar
3/4 c. oil
2 t. vanilla extract
2 c. all-purpose flour
2/3 c. baking cocoa
1/2 t. baking powder
1 t. baking soda
1 t. salt
3/4 c. milk chocolate chips

Combine zucchini, eggs, sugar, oil and vanilla. Add flour, cocoa, baking powder, baking soda and salt; stir in chocolate chips. Fill paper-lined muffin cups 2/3 full. Bake at 325 degrees for 25 minutes, or until a toothpick inserted near center tests clean. Cool in tin 5 minutes. Remove from tin; cool completely. Frost with Peanut Butter Frosting. Makes 2 dozen.

Peanut Butter Frosting:

1/2 c. creamy peanut butter
1/3 c. butter, softened
1 T. milk
1/2 t. vanilla extract
1-1/2 c. powdered sugar

Beat peanut butter, butter, milk and vanilla until smooth. Gradually beat in powdered sugar.

Yummy Spice Cupcakes

Brenda Stocks
Preston, ID

If raisins aren't your favorite, try milk chocolate chips.

2 c. all-purpose flour
1 t. baking soda
1/2 t. baking powder
1/2 t. cinnamon
1 t. pumpkin pie spice
1/2 t. salt
1 c. sugar
1/2 c. butter, melted
15-oz. jar applesauce
Optional: 1/2 c. raisins

In a bowl, combine flour, baking soda, baking powder and spices. Stir in sugar and butter. Mix in applesauce until well combined. Stir in raisins, if using. Fill greased muffin cups 2/3 full. Bake at 350 degrees for 20 to 25 minutes, until a toothpick tests clean. Cool completely. Frost with Vanilla Butter Cream Frosting. Makes 1-1/2 dozen.

Vanilla Butter Cream Frosting:

1/2 c. butter, softened
4 c. powdered sugar
1/2 t. salt
1/3 c. milk
1 t. vanilla extract

In a large bowl, beat butter until smooth. Add remaining ingredients; mix until smooth and creamy.

Pineapple-Orange Cakes

18-1/4 oz. pkg. pineapple
  cake mix
11-oz. can mandarin oranges
4 eggs, beaten
1/2 c. sour cream

In a large bowl, combine dry cake mix, oranges with juice, eggs and sour cream. Beat with an electric mixer on medium speed for 2 minutes. Fill greased muffin cups 2/3 full. Bake at 350 degrees for 20 minutes, or until a toothpick tests clean. Cool in tin on wire racks 5 minutes. Remove from tin and cool completely. Frost cupcakes with Orange Frosting. Refrigerate until ready to serve. Makes 2 dozen.

Orange Frosting:
4-oz. cream cheese, softened
1/4 c. butter, softened
1-1/2 t. orange zest
4-1/2 t. orange juice
3 c. powdered sugar

In a large bowl, beat cream cheese and butter with an electric mixer at medium speed until creamy. Beat in orange zest and juice until combined. Gradually beat in powdered sugar until smooth.

27

Michelle Campen
Peoria, IL

My friend made me these cupcakes...they were so good, I had to ask her for the recipe!

Strawberry Cupcake Cones

2 c. all-purpose flour
1/2 c. sugar
2 t. baking powder
1/2 t. baking soda
1/2 t. salt
2 eggs, beaten
6-oz. container whipped-style
   strawberry yogurt
1/2 c. oil
1/2 t. strawberry extract
1 c. strawberries, hulled and
   chopped
15 flat-bottomed ice cream cones
Optional: chocolate frosting
Garnish: sprinkles

Combine flour, sugar, baking powder, baking soda and salt. In another bowl, beat eggs, yogurt, oil, extract and strawberries. Stir egg mixture into flour mixture just until combined. Spoon 2 tablespoons batter into each cone. Place cones in ungreased muffin cups. Bake at 375 degrees for 18 to 20 minutes; let cool. Decorate with frosting or Chocolate Glaze; garnish as desired. Makes 15.

Chocolate Glaze:

1 c. semi-sweet chocolate chips
1 T. shortening

Melt ingredients together over low heat and stir until smooth.

Jackie Smulski
Lyons, IL
You don't have to worry about melting or spills with these cones. Sure to disappear fast!

Tiny Turtle Cupcakes

21-1/2 oz. pkg. brownie mix
1/2 c. pecans, chopped
16-oz. container dark chocolate
    fudge frosting
1/2 c. pecans, toasted and
    coarsely chopped

Prepare brownie batter according to package directions. Stir in chopped pecans. Fill paper-lined mini muffin cups 2/3 full. Bake at 350 degrees for 18 minutes, or until a toothpick tests clean. Cool cupcakes in tins on wire racks 5 minutes. Remove from tins; cool completely. Frost cupcakes; top with toasted pecans. Spoon Caramel Sauce evenly over cupcakes. Store in refrigerator. Makes 4-1/2 dozen.

Caramel Sauce:

12 caramels, unwrapped
1 to 2 T. whipping cream

Combine caramels and one tablespoon cream in a small saucepan; cook and stir over low heat until smooth. Add remaining cream as needed for desired consistency.

29

Teresa Podracky
Solon, OH
I give these little chocolate bites to my kids' soccer coaches for an end-of-the-season gift...and keep some for myself, too!

Mini Mousse Cupcakes

2-1/3 c. milk chocolate chips
6 eggs, beaten
1/4 c. plus 2 T. all-purpose flour
Garnish: whipped cream,
  chocolate shavings

Melt chocolate in a double boiler over medium heat and let cool slightly. In a large bowl, beat eggs and flour. Beat in melted chocolate until combined. Fill paper-lined mini muffin cups 2/3 full. Bake at 325 degrees for 7 to 10 minutes, until edges are done and centers shake slightly. Cool in tin on wire rack for 20 minutes. Remove from tin; cool completely. Garnish with whipped cream and chocolate shavings. Makes about 2 dozen.

Vickie
Chocolate lovers will swoon over these delectable cakes!

Sweet Angel Cupcakes

16-oz. pkg. angel food cake mix
2 T. poppy seed
1-1/2 t. almond extract, divided
1/2 c. sliced almonds, chopped
1-1/2 c. powdered sugar
1 T. plus 2 t. water

Prepare cake mix according to package directions, adding poppy seed and one teaspoon extract to batter. Fill paper-lined muffin cups 2/3 full. Sprinkle batter with almonds. Bake at 350 degrees for 15 to 20 minutes, until tops are golden. Let cool completely. Combine powdered sugar, water and remaining extract, stirring until smooth. Drizzle icing over cupcakes. Makes 2-1/2 dozen.

Roxanne Vilhauer
Springfield, MO
Put several cupcakes in a tea towel-lined basket with a note that reads, "You're an angel!" A sweet thank-you for a friend.

Snickerdoodle Cupcakes

18-1/4 oz. pkg. white cake mix
1 c. milk
1/2 c. butter, melted and cooled
   slightly
3 eggs, beaten
1 t. vanilla extract
2 t. cinnamon

In a large bowl, combine dry cake mix
and remaining ingredients. Beat with
an electric mixer on low speed for
3 minutes. Fill greased muffin cups
2/3 full. Bake at 350 degrees for 22 to
25 minutes. Let cool. Frost with
Cinnamon Frosting. Makes one dozen.

Cinnamon Frosting:

1/2 c. butter, softened
1 t. vanilla extract
1 T. cinnamon
3-3/4 c. powdered sugar
3 to 4 T. milk

Beat butter until fluffy. Mix in vanilla,
cinnamon and powdered sugar. Stir in
enough milk for desired consistency.

Diana Bulls
Reedley, CA
An easy and delicious
version of an all-time
favorite cookie!

Lemonade Cupcakes

1/2 c. frozen lemonade
  concentrate, thawed
18-1/4 oz. pkg. white cake mix
8-oz. container sour cream
3-oz. pkg. cream cheese, softened
3 eggs, beaten
2 T. lemon zest
Optional: lemon drops

In a bowl, combine all ingredients except lemon drops. Beat with an electric mixer on low speed for 3 minutes. Fill paper-lined muffin cups 2/3 full. Bake at 350 degrees for 22 minutes, or until a toothpick tests clean. Frost with Cream Cheese Frosting; garnish with lemon drops, if desired. Makes 2-1/2 dozen.

Cream Cheese Frosting:

8-oz. pkg. cream cheese,
  softened
1/2 c. butter, softened
2 t. vanilla extract
16-oz. pkg. powdered sugar

Beat together cream cheese and butter until smooth. Blend in vanilla. Gradually beat in powdered sugar.

**Sandy Roy
Crestwood, KY**

Offer these little cakes at your lemonade stand and watch the customers line up!

Toasted Coconut Cupcakes

8-oz. pkg. white cake mix
1 t. cinnamon
1/3 c. butter, softened
1 c. sugar
1 egg, beaten
1 t. vanilla extract
3/4 c. milk

Combine dry cake mix and cinnamon in a bowl; set aside. Blend butter and sugar; mix in egg and vanilla. Beat into the cake mixture alternately with milk. Fill paper-lined muffin cups half full. Bake at 350 degrees for 20 to 25 minutes. Let cool slightly. While cupcakes are warm in the tin, spread 2 teaspoons Coconut Frosting onto the center of each; don't spread to edges. Broil cupcakes in tin until coconut is lightly toasted, about 2 to 3 minutes. Makes one dozen.

Coconut Frosting:

1/4 c. butter, softened
1/3 c. brown sugar, packed
2 T. milk
1 c. sweetened flaked coconut
1 t. cinnamon

Combine butter and brown sugar. Blend in remaining ingredients.

Kerry Mayer
Dunham Springs, LA
My sister, Vanessa, made these amazing cupcakes for a church bake sale and they were a tremendous success.

Peanut Butter Cup Cupcakes

1/3 c. butter, softened
1/3 c. creamy peanut butter
1-1/4 c. brown sugar, packed
2 eggs, beaten
1 t. vanilla extract
1-3/4 c. all-purpose flour
1-3/4 t. baking powder
1 t. salt
1 c. milk
16 mini peanut butter cups

In a bowl, combine butter, peanut butter and brown sugar. Beat in eggs and vanilla. Combine flour, baking powder and salt; add to butter mixture alternately with milk. Fill paper-lined muffin cups half full. Press a peanut butter cup into the center of each, until top edge is even with batter. Bake at 350 degrees for 22 to 24 minutes, until a toothpick inserted on an angle toward the center tests clean. Cool in tin on wire rack 10 minutes. Remove from tin and cool completely. Makes 16.

35

Kathy Murphy
Lawrence, NE

I serve these at Sunday morning coffee time at church. There are never any leftovers!

Madelene's Buttermilk-Molasses Cookies

1-1/2 c. sugar, divided
1 c. shortening
1 c. light molasses
1 c. buttermilk
1 t. vanilla extract
5 c. all-purpose flour
4 t. baking soda
1/2 t. salt
1/2 t. ground ginger
1/2 t. cinnamon
Optional: 1 c. raisins

In a bowl, beat together one cup sugar, shortening, molasses, buttermilk and vanilla. In another bowl, combine flour, baking soda, salt and spices. Stir flour mixture into sugar mixture; mix in raisins, if desired. Drop by rounded teaspoonfuls 2 inches apart on greased baking sheets. Sprinkle with remaining sugar to cover. Bake at 350 degrees for 12 to 15 minutes. Makes 2 to 3 dozen.

Casey Tabolt
Pulaski, NY

My grandmother would make these cookies and then call our house. We went right over so we could eat them warm out of the oven!

Iced Carrot Cookies

1 c. butter, softened
3/4 c. sugar
1 egg, beaten
1 c. carrot, peeled, cooked
   and mashed
2 c. all-purpose flour
2 t. baking powder
1/2 t. salt
1 t. vanilla extract
3 to 4 drops almond extract

Blend together butter and sugar;
add egg and carrots. In a separate
bowl, sift together flour, baking
powder and salt; add to butter
mixture, blending well. Stir
in extracts. Drop by teaspoonfuls
onto greased baking sheets. Bake at
375 degrees for 10 minutes, or until
just lightly golden. Let cool and frost
with Citrus Icing. Makes 3 dozen.

Citrus Icing:

1/4 c. butter, softened
2 c. powdered sugar
3 T. orange or lemon juice
1 T. orange or lemon zest

Blend butter and powdered sugar.
Add juice and zest; mix well.

**Paula Purcell
Plymouth Meeting, PA**
One of my daughter's favorite
stories was *Rabbit Finds a
Way*, about a bunny who loved
goodies made with carrots.
Erin wanted these cookies
whenever we read the story!

Double Chocolate Cookies

1 c. sugar
1 c. brown sugar, packed
1 c. butter, softened
2 eggs, beaten
1 t. baking soda
1 t. cream of tartar
1/2 t. salt
2 c. all-purpose flour
1/2 c. baking cocoa
1 c. semi-sweet chocolate chips
Garnish: additional sugar

In a large bowl, mix sugar, brown sugar, butter and eggs. In another bowl, whisk remaining ingredients except chocolate chips and garnish. Add flour mixture to sugar mixture and combine until well blended. Stir in chocolate chips. Form dough into one-inch balls; roll in additional sugar. Place on ungreased baking sheets. Bake at 350 degrees for 8 to 10 minutes. Makes 3 dozen.

Kristi Watson
Highland Ranch, CO
Doubly delectable!
For variety, use white
chocolate chips.

Tasty Cookie Pops

1/2 c. butter, softened
1/2 c. shortening
1 c. sugar
1 c. powdered sugar
2 eggs, beaten
3/4 c. oil
2 t. vanilla extract
4 c. all-purpose flour
1 t. baking soda
1 t. salt
1 t. cream of tartar
Garnish: sprinkles
lollipop sticks

Beat butter and shortening until fluffy; add sugars, beating well. Beat in eggs, oil and vanilla. In a separate bowl, combine flour and remaining ingredients except sprinkles. Cover and chill 2 hours. Shape dough into 1-1/2 inch balls. Roll each ball in sprinkles, pressing gently, if needed, to coat. Place 2 inches apart on ungreased baking sheets. Insert a stick about one inch into each ball. Bake at 350 degrees for 10 to 11 minutes, until set. Let cool 2 minutes on baking sheets; cool completely on wire racks. Makes 4-1/2 dozen.

**Claire Bertram
Lexington, KY**
Ever since I discovered these pops, I've been making them for every special occasion!

Brown Sugar-Apple Cookies

1 c. brown sugar, packed
2 eggs, beaten
1/2 t. baking soda
1 t. cinnamon
1/2 t. salt
1/2 c. shortening
2 t. vanilla extract
2 c. all-purpose flour
1 c. apples, cored, peeled and
    sliced

Mix together all ingredients, stirring
in apples last. Drop by teaspoonfuls
onto ungreased baking sheets. Bake at
350 degrees for 8 to 10 minutes. Makes
3-1/2 to 4 dozen.

Nancy Hannon
Lewistown, PA

Perfect for sharing with
friends over a steamy pot
of spiced tea.

Winslow Whoopie Pies

1/3 c. baking cocoa
1 c. sugar
1 egg, beaten
1/3 c. shortening, melted and
  cooled
3/4 c. milk
2 c. all-purpose flour
1 t. baking soda
1/8 t. salt
1 t. vanilla extract
Optional: chocolate sprinkles

In a bowl, combine cocoa and sugar. In another bowl, beat egg and shortening; add to cocoa mixture and stir in remaining ingredients except sprinkles. Drop by rounded tablespoonfuls onto lightly greased baking sheets. Bake at 350 degrees for 15 minutes. Let cool. Frost the flat sides of half the cookies with Marshmallow Filling; top with remaining cookies. Roll edges in sprinkles, if using. Makes one dozen.

Marshmallow Filling:

2 c. powdered sugar
2/3 c. shortening
2 T. milk
6 T. marshmallow creme
1 t. vanilla extract

Combine all ingredients; stir until smooth.

Carissa Ellerd
Thomaston, ME

This yummy and often-requested family recipe is a huge hit at any social gathering. I like to tint the filling with food coloring to match the occasion!

41

Oh-So-Fun Fortune Cookies

Your baking talents win the applause of others.

**Karen Ensign
Providence, UT**

These are the best-tasting fortune cookies! I add in jokes or fun fortunes and give them out as gifts... people love them!

3 egg whites, beaten
3/4 c. sugar
1/8 t. salt
1/4 c. canola oil
1/2 t. vanilla extract
1/2 t. almond extract
1 T. water
1 c. all-purpose flour
3-inch by 1/2-inch paper fortunes

Mix egg whites, sugar and salt. Add remaining ingredients except fortunes; mix thoroughly. Batter will be very thin. Make 2 cookies at a time, otherwise, the cookies will harden before you can shape them. Spray parchment paper-lined baking sheets with non-stick vegetable spray. Spread batter by teaspoonfuls onto greased baking sheets. Spread with the back of a spoon into 3 to 3-1/2 inch rounds. Bake at 350 degrees for 6 to 7 minutes, until edges are golden. Immediately place a paper fortune in center of cookie; fold in half carefully so cookie doesn't flatten. Pick up corners created by fold and fold them together. Place cookies in empty egg carton cups to cool. Makes about 2-1/2 dozen.

Pistachio Thumbprints

1 c. margarine, softened
1/3 c. powdered sugar
1 egg, beaten
1 t. vanilla extract
3/4 t. almond extract
2 c. all-purpose flour
3.4-oz. pkg. instant pistachio
  pudding mix
1 c. pecans, finely chopped
1/2 c. semi-sweet chocolate chips
2 t. shortening

Blend margarine, powdered sugar, egg and extracts. Stir in flour and dry pudding mix. Form dough into one-inch balls; roll in pecans. Place on greased baking sheets; gently press a thumbprint into each. Bake at 350 degrees for 10 to 12 minutes; let cool. Spoon Vanilla Filling into thumbprints. In a plastic zipping bag, microwave remaining ingredients until melted, one to 2 minutes, stirring every 15 seconds. Snip off tip of one corner; drizzle over cookies. Makes 3 dozen.

Vanilla Filling:

2 T. margarine, softened
2 c. powdered sugar
1 t. vanilla extract
2 T. milk

Combine all ingredients; mix well.

43

Shawna Green
Dumas, TX

My good friend, Lisa, is an awesome cook and shared this recipe with me. Everyone raves about these delicious cookies!

Giant Chocolate Malt Cookies

1 c. butter-flavored shortening
1-1/4 c. brown sugar, packed
1/2 c. malted milk powder
2 T. chocolate syrup
1 T. vanilla extract
1 egg, beaten
2 c. all-purpose flour
1 t. baking soda
1/2 t. salt
1-1/2 c. semi-sweet chocolate
   chunks
1 c. milk chocolate chips

In a large bowl, blend shortening, brown sugar, malted milk powder, syrup and vanilla for 2 minutes. Add egg; blend well and set aside. Mix together flour, baking soda and salt; gradually blend into shortening mixture. Fold in chocolates; shape dough into 2-inch balls. Arrange 3 inches apart on ungreased baking sheets; bake at 375 degrees for 12 to 14 minutes. Cool on baking sheets for 2 minutes before removing to a wire rack to cool completely. Makes 1-1/2 dozen.

Pat Habiger
Spearville, KS

The next best thing to a good old-fashioned malted shake!

Granny's Chocolate Fudge Cookies

2 6-oz. pkgs. semi-sweet
  chocolate chips
1/4 c. butter
14-oz. can sweetened condensed
  milk
1 t. vanilla extract
1 c. all-purpose flour
1 c. chopped nuts

In a microwave-safe bowl, combine
chocolate chips, butter and
condensed milk. Heat on high
setting until melted, stirring every
30 seconds. Add vanilla, flour and
nuts. Drop by teaspoonfuls onto
greased baking sheets. Bake at
350 degrees for 7 minutes, or until
golden. Cool on wire racks. Makes
5 to 6 dozen.

45

Karen Adams
Cincinnati, OH

My grandmother used to make
these for church dinners.
The food was awesome,
especially these cookies!

Hazelnut Pinwheels

1 c. butter, softened
1 c. sugar
2 egg yolks, beaten
1 t. vanilla extract
1 t. orange extract
1 t. orange zest
2 c. all-purpose flour
1/2 c. chocolate-hazelnut spread

Combine butter and sugar; beat until creamy. Stir in yolks and extracts. Stir in orange zest and flour. Refrigerate dough for 30 minutes. Roll out dough into two, 1/4-inch thick rectangles. Spread with chocolate-hazelnut spread, leaving a 1/4-inch border. Roll up the dough jelly-roll style. Refrigerate another 30 minutes. Slice the rolls into 1/2-inch slices. Arrange slices on ungreased baking sheets. Bake at 350 degrees for 12 to 15 minutes, until edges are slightly golden. Makes about 2 dozen.

Emily Puskac
New Cumberland, WV

Position dental floss under the roll, bring up the floss ends, cross over the center and gently pull to cut the slices...easy!

Rainbow Swirl Cookies

3/4 c. butter, softened
3-oz. pkg. cream cheese,
  softened
1 c. sugar
1 egg, beaten
1 t. vanilla extract
2-3/4 c. all-purpose flour
1 t. baking powder
1/4 t. salt
purple, blue, yellow and pink
  gel paste colorings
12 lollipop sticks

In a bowl, beat butter, cream cheese and sugar until fluffy. Add egg and vanilla; beat until smooth and set aside. Combine flour, baking powder and salt; add to butter mixture. Stir until soft dough forms. Divide dough into fourths. Tint each with a different food color. Wrap in plastic wrap and chill for 2 hours. Roll dough into 3/4-inch balls. For each cookie, place one ball of each color together and roll to make one large ball. Shape into a 12-inch-long rope; starting at one end, coil rope to make a 2-3/4 inch round cookie. Place 3 inches apart on lightly greased baking sheets. Insert lollipop sticks into bottoms of cookies. Bake at 350 degrees for 8 to 10 minutes, until lightly golden. Makes one dozen.

Jamie Johnson
Gooseberry Patch

So pretty and playful! For the most vibrant colors, use gel paste food coloring found in craft stores.

Simple Almond Biscotti

2 c. butter, softened
3/4 c. sugar
2 eggs, beaten
3 T. orange zest
1 t. almond extract
2-1/4 c. all-purpose flour
1-1/2 t. baking powder
1/4 t. salt
3/4 c. slivered almonds, toasted

In a large bowl, beat together butter and sugar; add eggs. Mix in orange zest and almond extract until well blended. Stir in remaining ingredients. On a floured board, divide dough in half; roll and form each half into a 10-inch by 1-1/2 inch roll. Arrange rolls on an ungreased baking sheet 2 inches apart. Bake at 350 degrees for 20 to 25 minutes. Let cool on baking sheet for 5 minutes. Slice each roll diagonally into 1/2-inch thick slices. Lay the slices cut-side down on the baking sheet; bake for an additional 8 minutes. Turn slices over and bake an additional 8 to 10 minutes, until lightly golden. Remove from baking sheet to cool on a wire rack. Makes 2 dozen.

Kelly Alderson
Erie, PA

Enjoy these crisp cookies as an on-the-go breakfast or an after-dinner sweet.

The Ultimate Chip Cookies

2-1/2 c. all-purpose flour
1 t. baking soda
1/2 t. salt
1 c. butter, softened
1 c. brown sugar, packed
1/2 c. sugar
2 eggs, beaten
1 T. vanilla extract
3/4 c. semi-sweet chocolate chips
3/4 c. white chocolate chips
3/4 c. peanut butter chips
3/4 c. candy-coated chocolate
   mini-baking bits
1/2 c. chopped pecans

49

Combine flour, baking soda and salt; set aside. In a large bowl, beat together butter and sugars until light and fluffy; blend in eggs and vanilla. Mix flour mixture into butter mixture; fold in chips, baking bits and pecans. Drop by tablespoonfuls 2 inches apart onto ungreased baking sheets; bake at 375 degrees for 10 to 12 minutes. Cool on baking sheets for 2 minutes; remove to wire racks to cool completely. Makes about 4 dozen.

Cindy Griffin
Bloomfield, MO
Bursting with flavor, these will be an instant hit!

Mint-Chocolate Sandwiches

1/4 c. whipping cream
12-oz. pkg. semi-sweet chocolate
  chips, divided
3/4 t. peppermint extract
2 9-oz. pkgs. chocolate wafer
  cookies

In a small saucepan, bring cream to a simmer over medium heat. Add 3/4 cup chocolate chips; stir constantly until melted and smooth. Stir in extract. Let cool 15 minutes. Spoon one teaspoon chocolate mixture onto a wafer cookie; sandwich with another cookie. Repeat with remaining cookies. Refrigerate for 10 minutes, or until firm. Melt remaining chocolate in a double boiler, stirring constantly. Let cool slightly. Dip each sandwich into melted chocolate to coat; shake off excess. Place sandwiches on a wire rack set over a baking sheet; refrigerate 15 minutes, or until set. Makes 3 dozen.

Carol Lytle
Columbus, OH

Crunchy, creamy, minty
goodness...yum!

The Best Oatmeal Cookies

1 c. golden raisins
3 eggs, beaten
1 t. vanilla extract
1/2 c. margarine, softened
1/2 c. butter, softened
1 c. brown sugar, packed
1 c. sugar
2-1/2 c. all-purpose flour
1 t. salt
2 t. baking soda
1 T. cinnamon
2 c. quick-cooking oats,
    uncooked
1 c. chopped pecans

In a small bowl, combine raisins,
eggs and vanilla. Cover with plastic
wrap and let stand one hour. In a
large bowl, combine margarine,
butter and sugars. In a separate bowl,
whisk together flour, salt, baking
soda and cinnamon. Add flour
mixture to margarine mixture; mix
until well blended. Stir in raisin
mixture, oats and pecans. Dough
will be stiff. Drop by rounded
teaspoonfuls onto ungreased baking
sheets. Bake at 350 degrees for 10 to
12 minutes. Makes 4 dozen.

Trudy Cox
Plano, TX

I just keep this recipe on
my e-mail for forwarding to
anyone who asks for it!
Soaking the raisins is what
makes them so special.

Blueberry Linzer Tarts

1-1/4 c. butter, softened
2/3 c. sugar
1-1/2 c. almonds, ground
1/8 t. cinnamon
2 c. all-purpose flour
6 T. blueberry preserves
Garnish: powdered sugar

Blend butter and sugar until light and fluffy. Stir in almonds, cinnamon and flour, 1/2 cup at a time. Cover and refrigerate for about one hour. On a lightly floured surface, roll out half of dough 1/8-inch thick. Cut out 24 circles with a 2-1/2 inch round cookie cutter. Cut out centers of 12 circles with a 1/2-inch mini cookie cutter; leave remaining 12 circles uncut. Arrange one inch apart on ungreased baking sheets. Bake at 325 degrees for 10 to 12 minutes, until golden. Cool completely on a wire rack. Thinly spread preserves over solid circles; sprinkle cut-out cookies with powdered sugar. Carefully sandwich solid and cut-out cookies together. Spoon a little of remaining jam into cut-outs. Makes one dozen.

Cathy Hillier
Salt Lake City, UT

Any flavor of preserves will work in these divine cookies!

Buttermilk Sugar Cookies

Meri Hebert
Cheboygan, MI
I make these for every holiday...they're the softest cookies ever, and everyone always wants the recipe!

2 c. sugar
2 c. shortening
4 eggs, beaten
1 T. vanilla extract
2 c. buttermilk
6 c. all-purpose flour
1 T. plus 1 t. baking powder
2 t. baking soda
1/2 t. salt
16-oz. container butter cream
   frosting
Optional: colored sugar
   or sprinkles

Blend together sugar, shortening and eggs. Add vanilla and buttermilk. In a separate bowl, combine flour, baking powder, baking soda and salt; stir into sugar mixture. Add more flour as needed to make a firm dough. Chill for 2 to 3 hours or overnight. On a floured surface, roll out dough to a 1/4-inch thickness. Cut out with cookie cutters; place on greased baking sheets. Bake at 350 degrees for 7 to 8 minutes. Let cool. Frost and decorate as desired. Makes about 6 dozen.

Coconut-Lime Macaroons

3 egg whites, beaten
3 c. sweetened flaked coconut
1/4 c. sugar
3 to 4 T. all-purpose flour
1/4 c. lime juice
1 to 2 T. lime zest
1/4 t. vanilla extract

In a large bowl, combine all ingredients
thoroughly. Form into one-inch balls
and place 1/2 inch apart on lightly
greased baking sheets. Bake at
350 degrees for 12 to 15 minutes,
until edges are lightly golden. Makes 2
to 3 dozen.

Sharon Demers
Dolores, CO

I experimented and came
up with this macaroon
alternative. The taste is
refreshing and perfect for
a summer get-together
or ladies' tea.

Macadamia & Chocolate Chip Cookies

2-1/2 c. all-purpose flour
1 t. baking soda
1/2 t. salt
3/4 c. sugar
3/4 c. brown sugar, packed
1 c. margarine
1-1/2 t. vanilla extract
2 eggs, beaten
2 c. extra-large milk chocolate
   chips or chunks
3/4 c. macadamia nuts, chopped
Optional: 1/2 c. sweetened
   flaked coconut

55

Mix together flour, baking soda
and salt; set aside. In a large bowl,
combine sugars; beat in margarine
and vanilla until fluffy. Add eggs,
mixing well. Add flour mixture to
sugar mixture and beat until well
blended. Stir in chocolate chips,
macadamia nuts and coconut, if
using. Drop by 1/4 cupfuls, 3 inches
apart, onto ungreased baking sheets.
Bake at 375 degrees for 10 to
15 minutes, until golden. Makes
2 to 3 dozen.

Elizabeth Arnold
Dallas, OR

A yummy recipe combining
two of my favorites...
milk chocolate and
macadamia nuts!

Italian Cheese Cookies

2 c. sugar
1 c. butter, softened
1 t. vanilla extract
1 t. salt
15-oz. container ricotta cheese
4 c. all-purpose flour
1 t. baking soda

Use an electric mixer on medium speed to blend sugar, butter, vanilla, salt and ricotta cheese. Gradually stir in flour; mix in baking soda. Drop by teaspoonfuls onto ungreased baking sheets. Bake at 350 degrees for 10 to 13 minutes. Cool on wire racks. Spread Sweet Vanilla Icing over cookies. Makes about 4 dozen.

Sweet Vanilla Icing:

2/3 c. plus 1 T. sweetened
   condensed milk
1/2 c. butter, softened
1 t. vanilla extract
2 c. powdered sugar
Optional: red food coloring

Mix all ingredients with an electric mixer on low speed.

Sue Scott
Palmerton, PA

A former co-worker gave me this recipe years ago...it has become one of my husband's favorites!

Baklava Cookies

1/4 c. butter
1/2 c. powdered sugar
3 T. honey
3/4 c. walnuts, finely chopped
1/4 t. cinnamon
1 t. lemon zest
18-oz. pkg. refrigerated sugar
  cookie dough

In a saucepan over low heat, melt butter; stir in powdered sugar and honey. Bring to a boil and remove from heat. Stir in nuts, cinnamon and lemon zest. Let cool 30 minutes. Shape cooled butter mixture into 1/2-inch balls. Divide cookie dough into 24 pieces. Roll each piece of dough into a ball and place 2 inches apart on greased baking sheets. Bake at 350 degrees for 6 minutes. Remove cookies and press a butter-mixture ball into the center of each cookie. Bake an additional 6 to 7 minutes, until edges are golden. Transfer to wire racks and cool completely. Makes 2 dozen.

57

Tara Horton
Gooseberry Patch

All the wonderful flavor of baklava without all the work!

Twist Cookies

1 c. butter, softened
1-1/2 c. sugar
6 eggs, divided
1 t. vanilla extract
4 t. baking powder
4 to 5 c. all-purpose flour
Optional: sanding sugar

With an electric mixer on high speed, beat butter until fluffy, 4 to 5 minutes. Gradually add sugar, beating another 5 minutes. Add 4 eggs, one at a time, mixing well after each addition; blend in vanilla and baking powder. Gradually mix in flour until a stiff dough forms; roll dough into one-inch balls. Roll each ball into an 8-inch-long rope; fold in half and twist 2 to 3 times. Place on aluminum foil-lined baking sheets; set aside. Beat remaining eggs; brush onto each twist. Sprinkle with sugar, if using. Bake at 350 degrees for 15 to 20 minutes. Makes about 5 dozen.

Virginia Cook
Fairfield, CT

The prettiest cookies... sprinkle with colored sugar for extra sparkle.

Raspberry-Almond Shortbread Cookies

2/3 c. sugar
1 c. butter, softened
2 t. almond extract, divided
2 c. all-purpose flour
1/2 c. seedless raspberry jam
1 c. powdered sugar
2 to 3 t. water

Using an electric mixer on medium speed, combine sugar, butter and 1/2 teaspoon almond extract until creamy. Reduce speed to low and add flour. Continue beating until well mixed. Shape dough into one-inch balls. Place 2 inches apart on ungreased baking sheets. Gently press a thumbprint in center of each cookie. Fill each with about 1/4 teaspoon jam. Bake at 350 degrees for 14 to 18 minutes, until edges are lightly golden. Let cool one minute on baking sheets. Remove cookies to wire racks to cool completely. Combine remaining extract, powdered sugar and water; drizzle lightly over cookies. Makes 3-1/2 dozen.

Dee Ann Ice
Delaware, OH

These buttery-delicious cookies look beautiful on a dessert tray!

59

Maple Drop Cookies

1 c. butter, softened
3/4 c. sugar
2 c. all-purpose flour
1/4 t. salt
1-1/2 t. maple flavoring
Optional: pecan halves

Beat butter and sugar until light and fluffy; blend in remaining ingredients except pecan halves. Drop by teaspoonfuls onto greased baking sheets; press a pecan half on top of each cookie, if desired. Bake at 350 degrees for 12 to 15 minutes. Makes about 3 dozen.

Debi DeVore
Dover, OH

So easy! Sometimes we frost with cream cheese frosting flavored with a few drops of maple flavoring.

Chocolate-Orange Snowballs

9-oz. pkg. vanilla wafers
2-1/4 c. powdered sugar, divided
1/4 c. baking cocoa
1/4 c. light corn syrup
1/3 c. frozen orange juice
    concentrate, thawed
1-1/2 c. chopped pecans

In a food processor, combine vanilla wafers, 2 cups powdered sugar, cocoa, corn syrup and orange juice. Process until wafers are finely ground and mixture is well blended. Add pecans and process until nuts are finely chopped. Transfer mixture to a bowl; form into one-inch balls. Roll in remaining powdered sugar. Store in an airtight container. Makes about 5 dozen.

61

Beth Kramer
Port Saint Lucie, FL
I love the flavor combination of these no-bake snowballs. I'm in heaven with a cup of orange and spice tea!

Ice Cream Nut Roll Crescents

4 c. all-purpose flour
2 c. butter, softened
1 pt. vanilla ice cream, softened
3/4 c. milk
2 8-oz. pkgs. walnuts, finely
   chopped
1 c. sugar
1 t. vanilla extract
Garnish: powdered sugar

Combine flour, butter and ice cream.
Form dough into 4 balls; wrap in
plastic wrap and refrigerate 8 hours. In
a saucepan, heat milk just to boiling; let
cool slightly. In a bowl, combine milk,
walnuts, sugar and vanilla; thin with
one to 2 teaspoons milk if too thick.
Turn a dough ball out onto a powdered
sugar-covered surface. Roll dough into
a circle, 1/8-inch thick. Use a pizza
cutter to cut circle into 12 wedges.
Spread about 2 teaspoons walnut
mixture onto each slice; don't overfill.
Starting on the wide end, roll up each
wedge and form into a crescent shape.
Repeat for remaining dough balls.
Arrange crescents on ungreased baking
sheets. Bake at 350 degrees for 18 to
20 minutes. Sprinkle with powdered
sugar while still warm. Let cool. Store
in an airtight container. Makes 4 dozen.

Mel Chencharick
Julian, PA

The ice cream makes
these cookies so rich
and delicious.

Peanut Butter Sandwich Dips

Linda Doyle
West Seneca, NY
My grandchildren love these!
I've kept the recipe a secret
so they can always enjoy
them when they come to
visit Grandma & Grandpa.

1-1/2 c. all-purpose flour
3/4 t. baking soda
1/4 t. salt
1/2 c. butter, softened
1-1/4 c. creamy peanut butter,
   divided
1 c. sugar
1 egg, beaten
1/4 c. powdered sugar
1 c. semi-sweet chocolate chips
4 t. oil

Whisk together flour, baking soda
and salt. In a separate bowl, beat
butter, 1/2 cup peanut butter, sugar
and egg until smooth. Gradually beat
flour mixture into butter mixture.
Drop by rounded teaspoonfuls onto
ungreased baking sheets. Bake at
350 degrees for 10 minutes, or until
puffed. Cool 2 minutes on baking
sheets. Remove cookies to a wire rack;
let cool. Combine powdered sugar
with remaining peanut butter; spread
one rounded teaspoon on flat side of
half the cookies. Top with remaining
cookies. Refrigerate 30 minutes. In
a microwave-safe bowl, microwave
chocolate chips and oil one minute;
stir until melted. Dip cookies halfway
into melted chocolate. Let excess
drip off. Refrigerate on wax paper-
lined baking sheets until set. Makes
3 dozen.

63

Molasses Crinkles

3/4 c. shortening
1 c. brown sugar, packed
1 egg, beaten
1/4 c. molasses
2-1/4 c. all-purpose flour
1/4 t. baking soda
1 t. cinnamon
1 t. ground ginger
Garnish: sugar

In a bowl, mix shortening, brown sugar, egg and molasses. Stir in remaining ingredients except garnish in the order listed. Roll dough into one-inch balls. Dip tops in sugar and place on ungreased baking sheets. Gently press a thumbprint into each. Sprinkle one to 4 drops of water in each indentation. Bake at 350 degrees for 10 to 12 minutes. Let cool on a wire rack. Makes 4 dozen.

**Patty Fosnight
Childress, TX**

These are a favorite of all who taste them. My mother-in-law and I would make them every year to give away with our holiday cookie trays.

Triple-Layered Brownies

20-oz. pkg. brownie mix
3 eggs, beaten
1/4 c. water
1/2 c. oil
16-oz. container cream cheese
   frosting
1 c. creamy peanut butter
12-oz. pkg. milk chocolate chips
2-1/2 c. crispy rice cereal

In a large bowl, stir dry brownie mix, eggs, water and oil just until combined. Grease the bottom of a 13"x9" glass baking pan; pour in batter. Bake at 350 degrees for 27 to 30 minutes. Cool in pan. Spread frosting over cooled brownies; refrigerate until set. In a saucepan, melt peanut butter and chocolate chips together over low heat, stirring frequently until smooth. Remove from heat. Mix in cereal and spread evenly over frosting. Refrigerate until set. Cut into squares. Makes 2 dozen.

65

**Alicia Allen
Lakeside, AZ**

I make these cake-type brownies for any get-together. Everyone begs for the recipe! Be sure to use creamy frosting instead of whipped.

Divine Praline Brownies

22-1/2 oz. pkg. brownie mix
1/4 c. butter
1 c. brown sugar, packed
1 c. chopped pecans

Prepare brownie mix according to package directions. Spread in a greased 13"x9" baking pan. Set aside. Melt butter in a skillet over low heat; add brown sugar and pecans. Heat until sugar dissolves; drizzle over brownie mix. Bake at 350 degrees for 25 to 30 minutes. Cool and cut into bars. Keep refrigerated. Makes 12 to 15.

Sandy Bernards
Valencia, CA

Sugar-coated pecans give brownies a delicious new taste!

Gingerbread Brownies

1-1/2 c. all-purpose flour
1 c. sugar
1/2 t. baking soda
1/4 c. baking cocoa
1 t. ground ginger
1 t. cinnamon
1/2 t. ground cloves
1/4 c. butter, melted and slightly
   cooled
1/3 c. molasses
2 eggs, beaten
Garnish: powdered sugar

67

In a large bowl, combine flour, sugar, baking soda, cocoa and spices. In another bowl, combine butter, molasses and eggs. Add butter mixture to flour mixture, stirring until just combined. Spread in a greased 13"x9" baking pan. Bake at 350 degrees for 20 minutes. Cool in pan on a wire rack. Dust with powdered sugar. Cut into squares. Makes 2 dozen.

Stephanie Mayer
Portsmouth, VA
These brownies hit the spot when I've got a hankering for gingerbread but don't want to roll out cookie dough!

Pumpkin Spice & Chocolate Bars

2 eggs, beaten
1/2 c. oil
18-1/2 oz. pkg. yellow cake mix
1 t. pumpkin pie spice
1-1/2 c. semi-sweet chocolate chips
1/2 c. chopped nuts

In a bowl, combine eggs and oil. Stir in dry cake mix and pumpkin pie spice until well blended. Fold in chocolate chips and nuts. Spread into a greased 13"x9" baking pan. Bake at 350 degrees for 28 to 30 minutes. Cool completely. Cut into bars. Makes 20.

Kristin Pittis
Dennison, OH

This is a quick & easy dessert that can be made in a pinch. The pumpkin pie spice makes it a little different from traditional chocolate chip bars.

Cream Cheese Crescent Bars

2 8-oz. tubes refrigerated
    crescent rolls, separated
2 8-oz. pkgs. cream cheese,
    softened
1 t. vanilla extract
2/3 c. sugar
1 egg, separated

Line the bottom of a greased
13"x9" baking pan with one package
crescent rolls, pinching seams
together; set aside. Blend together
cream cheese, vanilla, sugar and
egg yolk; spread evenly over crust.
Gently place remaining crescent
roll dough on top, pinching together
seams. In a bowl, whisk egg white
until frothy; brush over dough.
Sprinkle with Cinnamon Topping;
bake at 350 degrees until golden,
about 25 to 30 minutes. Cool; slice
into bars or triangles. Makes 2 dozen.

Cinnamon Topping:

1/2 c. sugar
1/4 c. chopped pecans
1 t. cinnamon

Gently toss together all ingredients.

Lisa Delisi
Bristol, WI
I take this dessert to almost
every event I attend...and I
always bring copies of the
recipe because I get so
many requests!

69

Double Chocolate-Mint Brownies

1 c. all-purpose flour
1 c. sugar
1 c. plus 6 T. butter, softened
  and divided
4 eggs, beaten
16-oz. can chocolate syrup
2 c. powdered sugar
1 T. water
1/2 t. mint extract
3 drops green food coloring
1 c. semi-sweet chocolate chips

Beat flour, sugar, 1/2 cup butter, eggs and syrup in a large bowl until smooth; pour into a greased 13"x9" baking pan. Bake at 350 degrees for 25 to 30 minutes, until top springs back when lightly touched. Cool completely in pan. Combine powdered sugar and 1/2 cup butter, water, mint extract and food coloring in a bowl; beat until smooth. Spread over brownies; chill. Melt chocolate chips and remaining butter in a double boiler; stir until smooth. Pour over chilled mint layer; cover and chill until set. Cut into small squares to serve. Makes about 4 dozen.

Amy Gitter
Fond du Lac, WI
These fantastic brownies are rich and chocolatey with a yummy layer of mint.

Red Velvet Bars

18-1/2 oz. pkg. red velvet
   cake mix
2 T. brown sugar, packed
1 t. baking cocoa
2 eggs, beaten
1/2 c. oil
1/2 t. vanilla extract
2 T. water
1 c. white chocolate chips
1/2 c. chopped pecans
Optional: whipped topping,
   additional chopped pecans

In a large bowl, combine dry cake
mix, brown sugar and cocoa. Stir in
eggs, oil, vanilla and water. Mix in
chocolate chips and pecans. Spray
a 13"x9" baking pan with non-stick
vegetable spray; spread in batter.
Bake at 350 degrees for 18 to
20 minutes. Cool and spread with
whipped topping and additional
pecans, if using. Cut into bars.
Makes 20.

Judy Jones
Chinquapin, NC

The bars are easy to
fix...plus they're tasty
and pretty!

Rocky Road Brownies

19-1/2 oz. pkg. fudge brownie mix
2 c. mini marshmallows, divided
12-oz. pkg. semi-sweet chocolate
   chips, divided
1 c. dry-roasted peanuts, divided

Prepare brownie mix according to package instructions; spread in a greased 13"x9" baking pan. Sprinkle one cup mini marshmallows, one cup chocolate chips and 1/2 cup peanuts over batter. Bake at 350 degrees for 28 to 30 minutes. Remove from oven; sprinkle with remaining marshmallows, peanuts and chocolate chips. Let cool completely before cutting into squares. Makes 2 to 3 dozen.

Sheryl Whited
Austin, TX

Ooey-gooey and guaranteed
to be the talk of
the potluck!

Mock Lemon Meringue Bars

16-1/2 oz. tube refrigerated sugar
  cookie dough
21-oz. can lemon pie filling
8-oz. pkg. cream cheese,
  softened
7-oz. jar marshmallow creme
6-oz. container French vanilla
  yogurt
8-oz. container frozen whipped
  topping, thawed

Break up cookie dough and press
into the bottom of a greased
13"x9" baking pan. Bake at
350 degrees for 20 to 25 minutes,
until edges are golden and center
is set. Let cool completely. Spread
pie filling over crust. In a large bowl,
use a wooden spoon to beat cream
cheese, marshmallow creme and
yogurt until well blended. Fold in
whipped topping. Spread over pie
filling, swirling to resemble meringue
topping. Refrigerate 2 hours. Cut
into bars. Store in refrigerator.
Makes 2 dozen.

Cathy Elgin
Saint Louis Park, MN
If you like lemon meringue
pie, you will love these
bars...so easy and
no measuring!

73

German Chocolate Cookie Bars

1 egg, beaten
1/2 c. margarine, melted and
    cooled
1/2 t. vanilla extract
18-1/2 oz. pkg. German chocolate
    cake mix
1 c. sweetened flaked coconut,
    divided
16-oz. container vanilla frosting

In a large bowl, beat egg, margarine
and vanilla; stir in dry cake mix and
1/2 cup coconut. Spray a 13"x9" baking
pan with non-stick vegetable spray.
Spread batter in pan. Bake at
350 degrees for 25 to 30 minutes.
Cool in pan 10 minutes. Meanwhile,
combine remaining coconut with
frosting. Lightly spread 1/2 cup frosting
over warm bars. Let cool completely;
frost with remaining frosting. Cut into
bars. Makes 20.

Sally Aken-Linke
Norfolk, NE
I like using Mexican-blend
vanilla extract for a richer
flavor. Lightly frosting the
bars while still warm seals
in the moisture...so tasty!

Dorothy's Raisin Bars

1 c. raisins
3/4 c. apple juice
2 T. shortening
1 c. all-purpose flour
1/2 t. salt
1/2 t. baking soda
1/2 t. baking powder
1 t. cinnamon
1/4 t. ground cloves
1/8 t. nutmeg
Optional: 1/4 c. chopped nuts

In a small saucepan over low heat, bring raisins, apple juice and shortening to a boil. Remove from heat and cool. Mix remaining ingredients in a bowl; stir in raisin mixture. Pour into a greased 8"x8" baking pan. Bake at 350 degrees for 35 to 40 minutes; remove from oven and cool. Cut into 2-inch squares; store in an airtight container. Makes 16.

Delinda Blakney
Dallas, GA

This is one of my mom's favorite recipes! Perfect for packing in lunches or taking along on a road trip.

Salted Nut Roll Bars

18-1/2 oz. pkg. yellow cake mix
1 egg, beaten
1/4 c. butter, melted and slightly
  cooled
3 c. mini marshmallows
10-oz. pkg. peanut butter chips
1/2 c. light corn syrup
1/2 c. butter, softened
1 t. vanilla extract
2 c. salted peanuts
2 c. crispy rice cereal

Combine dry cake mix, egg and
melted butter; press into a greased
13"x9" baking pan. Bake at 350 degrees
for 10 to 12 minutes. Sprinkle
marshmallows over baked crust; return
to oven and bake for 3 additional
minutes, or until marshmallows are
melted. In a saucepan over medium
heat, melt peanut butter chips, corn
syrup, butter and vanilla. Stir in nuts
and cereal. Spread mixture over
marshmallow layer. Chill briefly
until firm; cut into squares. Makes
2-1/2 dozen.

Sandy Groezinger
Stockton, IL

Salty, sweet, crunchy
and gooey...every
bite satisfies!

Coffee Cream Brownies

3 1-oz. sqs. unsweetened baking
   chocolate, chopped
1/2 c. plus 2 T. butter, softened
   and divided
2 eggs, beaten
1 c. sugar
1 t. vanilla extract
2/3 c. all-purpose flour
1/4 t. baking soda
1 t. instant coffee granules
1/3 c. plus 1 T. whipping cream,
   divided
1 c. powdered sugar
1 c. semi-sweet chocolate chips

77

In a saucepan over low heat, melt baking chocolate and 1/2 cup butter; let cool. In a bowl, beat eggs, sugar and vanilla. Stir in chocolate mixture. Combine flour and baking soda and add to the chocolate mixture. Spread in a greased 8"x8" baking pan. Bake at 350 degrees for 25 to 30 minutes. Let cool. In a bowl, stir coffee granules into one tablespoon cream until dissolved. Beat in remaining butter and powdered sugar until creamy; spread over brownies. In a saucepan over low heat, stir and melt chocolate chips and remaining cream until thickened. Spread over cream layer. Let set and cut into squares. Makes one dozen.

Jennifer Crisp
Abingdon, IL

Go ahead and serve
with a scoop of
ice cream...so good!

Swirled Peanut Butter Cheesecake Bars

Jen Stout
Blandon, PA
This is a rich and delicious dessert for all cheesecake lovers!

2 c. graham cracker crumbs
1/2 c. butter, melted
1-1/3 c. sugar
2 8-oz. pkgs. cream cheese, softened
1/4 c. all-purpose flour
12-oz. can evaporated milk
2 eggs, beaten
1 T. vanilla extract
6-oz. pkg. peanut butter & milk chocolate chips

Combine cracker crumbs, butter and 1/3 cup sugar. Press into the bottom of an ungreased 13"x9" baking pan. Beat cream cheese, remaining sugar and flour until smooth. Gradually beat in evaporated milk, eggs and vanilla. Reserve one cup cream cheese mixture; spread remaining mixture over crust. Microwave peanut butter & chocolate chips in a microwave-safe bowl on medium for one to 2 minutes; stir until smooth. Stir in reserved cream cheese mixture; pour over bars. Swirl mixtures with a spoon, pulling plain cream cheese mixture up to surface. Bake at 325 degrees for 40 to 45 minutes, until set. Cool on a wire rack; refrigerate until firm. Cut into bars. Makes 20.

Apple Brownies

1/2 c. butter, softened
1 c. sugar
1 t. vanilla extract
1 egg, beaten
1-1/2 c. all-purpose flour
1/2 t. baking soda
1/2 t. baking powder
1/2 t. nutmeg
1 c. apples, cored, peeled and
    chopped
1/2 c. chopped nuts

Beat together butter and sugar
until fluffy; stir in vanilla and egg.
In a small bowl, combine flour,
baking soda, baking powder and
nutmeg. Add flour mixture to butter
mixture and mix thoroughly. Fold
in apples and nuts. Spread in a
greased 10"x10" baking pan. Bake at
350 degrees for 30 to 35 minutes.
Cool and cut into squares. Makes
one dozen.

79

Ann Watson
Leverett, MA

For the tastiest brownies,
try using juicy Golden
Delicious or tangy
Jonagold apples.

Gail's Pumpkin Bars

4 eggs, beaten
1 c. oil
2 c. sugar
15-oz. can pumpkin
2 c. all-purpose flour
2 t. baking powder
1 t. baking soda
1/2 t. salt
2 t. cinnamon
1/2 t. ground ginger
1/2 t. nutmeg
1/2 t. ground cloves

Mix together eggs, oil, sugar and pumpkin in a large bowl. Add remaining ingredients and mix well; pour into a greased and floured 18"x12" jelly-roll pan. Bake at 350 degrees for 30 to 40 minutes, until a toothpick comes out clean. Let cool; frost and cut into bars. Makes 1-1/2 to 2 dozen.

Cream Cheese Frosting:

8-oz. pkg. cream cheese, softened
6 T. butter, softened
1 T. milk
1 t. vanilla extract
4 c. powdered sugar

Beat together cream cheese, butter, milk and vanilla; gradually stir in powdered sugar to a spreading consistency.

Lisa Thomsen
Rapid City, SD

Dip a mini cookie cutter into cinnamon and lightly press into the frosting... such a pretty touch!

Scrumptious Cranberry Blondies

1/2 c. butter, softened
1/2 c. sugar
1/2 c. brown sugar, packed
3/4 t. baking powder
1/4 t. baking soda
1/4 t. salt
2 eggs, beaten
1 t. vanilla extract
1 c. all-purpose flour
1/2 c. sweetened dried
   cranberries
1/2 c. white chocolate chips
1 c. fresh cranberries

81

In a large bowl, beat together butter, sugars, baking powder, baking soda and salt. Beat in eggs and vanilla. Mix in flour, dried cranberries and chocolate chips. Line a 9"x9" baking pan with aluminum foil, leaving a few inches on sides for handles; spray with non-stick vegetable spray. Spread dough in pan; lightly press fresh cranberries into dough. Bake at 350 degrees for 25 to 30 minutes, until a toothpick tests clean. Cool; lift foil to remove from pan. Cut into bars. Makes one dozen.

Audrey Lett
Newark, DE

I look forward to when cranberries are in season, just so I can make these yummy blondies!

Peanut Butter Brownies

1 c. creamy peanut butter
1/2 c. butter, softened
2 c. brown sugar, packed
3 eggs, beaten
1 t. vanilla extract
1 c. all-purpose flour
1/2 t. salt

In a large bowl, blend together peanut butter and butter. Beat in brown sugar, eggs and vanilla until light and fluffy. Blend in flour and salt. Spread into a greased 13"x9" baking pan; bake at 350 degrees for 30 to 35 minutes. Cool in pan; frost with Peanut Butter Frosting. Makes 16.

Peanut Butter Frosting:

2 c. creamy peanut butter
1 c. margarine
1 t. vanilla extract
1/8 t. salt
3 to 4 T. whipping cream
2 c. powdered sugar

Blend peanut butter and margarine until fluffy; gradually blend in remaining ingredients until smooth.

Naomi Cooper
Delaware, OH

A nice change of pace from chocolate brownies! Top with chocolate frosting for a whole new taste.

Iced Raspberry Delights

16-1/2 oz. tube refrigerated sugar
  cookie dough
1-1/4 c. white chocolate chunks,
  divided
12-oz. jar seedless raspberry jam
1 t. oil

Press dough into the bottom of an
ungreased 13"x9" baking pan. Evenly
press one cup chocolate chunks into
dough. Bake at 350 degrees for 16 to
20 minutes, until lightly golden.
Spread jam over crust; bake an
additional 10 minutes. Cool
completely. Cut into squares or use
a cookie cutter to cut into shapes.
Combine remaining chocolate and
oil in a plastic zipping bag.
Microwave 30 to 45 seconds; squeeze
bag until chocolate is melted. Snip
off tip of one corner and drizzle over
bars. Refrigerate until set. Makes
3 dozen.

Vickie

These irresistible treats
come together easily and
make a thoughtful gift
for someone special.

Cookies & Cream Brownies

1/2 c. baking cocoa
1/2 c. margarine, melted
3/4 c. sugar, divided
1/2 c. brown sugar, packed
3 eggs, divided
1/2 c. all-purpose flour
1 t. baking powder
1-1/2 t. vanilla extract, divided
12 chocolate sandwich cookies,
   crushed
8-oz. pkg. cream cheese, softened

In a large bowl, combine cocoa, margarine, 1/2 cup sugar and brown sugar; blend well. Add 2 eggs, one at a time, beating well after each addition. Combine flour and baking powder; stir into cocoa mixture. Stir in one teaspoon vanilla and cookie crumbs. Spread into a greased 11"x7" baking pan. In a small bowl, beat cream cheese and remaining sugar, egg and vanilla until smooth. Spoon cream cheese mixture over batter; cut through batter with a knife to swirl. Bake at 350 degrees for 25 to 30 minutes, until a toothpick inserted near the center comes out with moist crumbs. Cool completely. Cut into bars or into circles using a biscuit cutter. Makes 2 dozen.

**Mary Gage
Wakewood, CA**
Pour a frosty glass
of milk and dig in!

The Best Blondies

1 c. butter, melted and slightly
    cooled
2 c. brown sugar, packed
2 eggs, beaten
2 t. vanilla extract
2 c. all-purpose flour
1/2 t. baking powder
1/4 t. salt
1 c. chopped pecans
1 c. white chocolate chips
3/4 c. toffee or caramel
    baking bits

Line the bottom of a 12"x9" baking
pan with parchment paper. Spray
sides of pan with non-stick vegetable
spray and set aside. In a large bowl,
mix together butter and brown sugar.
Beat in eggs and vanilla until smooth.
Stir in flour, baking powder and salt;
mix in remaining ingredients. Pour
into prepared pan and spread evenly.
Bake at 375 degrees for 30 to
40 minutes, until set in the middle.
Allow to cool in pan before cutting
into bars. Makes one dozen.

Elizabeth Cisneros
Chino Hills, CA

For an extra-special dessert,
serve topped with a scoop
of butter brickle ice
cream...delicious!

Gooey Toffee Scotchies

18-1/2 oz. pkg. yellow cake mix
1/2 c. brown sugar, packed
1/2 c. butter, melted and slightly
   cooled
2 eggs, beaten
1 c. cashews, chopped
8-oz. pkg. toffee baking bits

In a bowl, combine dry cake mix, brown sugar, butter and eggs. Beat with an electric mixer on medium speed for one minute. Stir in cashews. Press mixture into the bottom of a greased 15"x10" jelly-roll pan; sprinkle with toffee bits. Bake at 350 degrees for 15 to 20 minutes, until a toothpick tests clean. Cool in pan and cut into bars or triangles. To serve, drizzle with warm Toffee Sauce. Makes about 2-1/2 dozen.

Toffee Sauce:

3/4 c. plus 1 T. dark brown sugar,
   packed
2 T. dark corn syrup
6 T. butter
2/3 c. whipping cream

In a saucepan over medium heat, bring sugar, syrup and butter to a boil. Cook for 2 minutes. Stir in cream and simmer an additional 2 minutes, or until sauce thickens. Keep warm.

Rhonda Reeder
Ellicott City, MD

I'm always looking for desserts with toffee in them. These delectable bars are my new favorites!

Chocolate-Caramel Brownies

21-oz. pkg. brownie mix
16-oz. container milk chocolate
    frosting
6 to 8 T. caramel ice cream
    topping
Optional: chopped nuts

Prepare brownie mix according to
package directions. Let cool. Mix
together frosting and ice cream
topping in a microwave-safe bowl.
Microwave on high for 45 seconds;
stir and spread over brownies. Top
with nuts, if desired. Makes 2 to
3 dozen.

Brynne Stevenson
Springfield, OH

What more can I
tell you...these
are wonderful!

Chocolate Chip Cheesecake Squares

2 16-1/2 oz. tubes refrigerated
   chocolate chip cookie dough
2 c. sugar
3 eggs, beaten
2 8-oz. pkgs. cream cheese,
   softened

Slice cookie dough into 1/4-inch thick slices. Arrange half the cookie dough slices in a greased 13"x9" baking pan; press together to form a crust. In a bowl, combine sugar, eggs and cream cheese; beat until smooth. Spread over crust. Arrange remaining cookie dough slices over cream cheese layer. Bake at 350 degrees for 45 minutes to one hour, until golden. Cool; cut into squares. Makes 15.

**Cindy Windle
White Hall, AR**

Everyone loves this easy-to-make recipe. When I take them to church potlucks and office events, there are never any leftovers!

Staycation Coconut-Lime Bars

2 c. all-purpose flour
1/4 c. sugar
1/8 t. salt
1/2 c. plus 2-1/2 T. butter
4 eggs, beaten
1 c. chopped almonds
2 c. brown sugar, packed
3 c. sweetened flaked coconut
1-1/2 c. powdered sugar
2 T. lime juice
2 t. lime zest

Combine flour, sugar and salt in a bowl. Cut in butter until mixture resembles coarse meal. Press into an ungreased 15"x10" jelly-roll pan. Bake at 350 degrees for 15 minutes, or until golden. Mix eggs, almonds, brown sugar and coconut until well blended; spread over crust. Bake an additional 30 minutes, or until set. Remove pan to a wire rack; loosen the edges with a metal spatula. Meanwhile, use a fork to combine powdered sugar, lime juice and zest. Working quickly, spread powdered sugar mixture over bars while still warm. Let cool and cut into bars. Makes 4 dozen.

Joan White
Malvern, PA

A tangy dessert that puts you in the mood for sandy beaches and warm breezes!

Apricot Layer Bars

1-3/4 c. quick-cooking oats,
   uncooked
1-3/4 c. all-purpose flour
1 c. brown sugar, packed
1 c. butter, softened
1/8 t. salt
12-oz. jar apricot preserves

Mix together oats, flour, brown sugar,
butter and salt. Press half of mixture
into a greased 8"x8" baking pan.
Spread preserves over the top; top
with remaining oat mixture. Bake at
350 degrees for 35 minutes. Let cool;
cut into squares. Makes one to
1-1/2 dozen.

Marilyn Rogers
Port Townsend, WA
A classic recipe...one bite
and you'll know why!

Triple Chocolatey Brownies

2-1/4 c. sugar, divided
2-1/2 c. all-purpose flour,
    divided
1/2 c. baking cocoa
1/2 t. salt
1 c. oil
4 eggs, beaten
1 T. vanilla extract, divided
1/2 c. butter, softened
1/2 c. brown sugar, packed
2 T. milk
2 c. semi-sweet chocolate chips,
    divided
1 T. shortening

91

Combine 2 cups sugar, 1-1/2 cups flour, cocoa and salt; add oil, eggs and 2 teaspoons vanilla. Beat with an electric mixer on medium speed for 3 minutes; pour into a greased 13"x9" baking pan. Bake at 350 degrees for 30 minutes; cool. Beat butter, brown sugar and remaining sugar; add milk and remaining vanilla. Blend in remaining flour until smooth and creamy; fold in one cup chocolate chips. Spread mixture over brownies; refrigerate until firm and cut into squares. Melt remaining chocolate chips and shortening in a double boiler; stir until smooth. Drizzle over brownies. Makes 3 dozen.

Valerie Beeching
Paw Paw, MI

Oh, my! There's chocolate in the brownie, the topping and the icing!

Luscious Banana Bars

1/2 c. butter, softened
1 c. sugar
1 egg, beaten
1 t. vanilla extract
1-1/2 c. bananas, mashed
1-1/2 c. all-purpose flour
1 t. baking powder
1 t. baking soda
1/2 t. salt
1/4 c. baking cocoa

Beat together butter and sugar; add egg and vanilla. Blend until thoroughly combined; mix in bananas. Set aside. Combine flour, baking powder, baking soda and salt; blend into banana mixture. Divide batter in half; add cocoa to one half. Pour vanilla batter into a greased 13"x9" baking pan; spoon chocolate batter on top. Cut through batters with a knife to swirl. Bake at 350 degrees for 25 minutes. Cool; cut into bars. Makes 2-1/2 to 3 dozen.

Barbara Buckley
Edwards, MS

Bananas and chocolate are a terrific combination!

Tiger's Eye Brownies

10-oz. pkg. peanut butter chips
1/2 c. margarine
1-2/3 c. sugar
1-1/4 c. all-purpose flour
1/2 t. salt
1/2 t. baking powder
3 eggs, beaten
1 c. dark or semi-sweet chocolate
  chips

In a saucepan over low heat, melt peanut butter chips and margarine together, stirring frequently until smooth. Remove from heat. Stir in remaining ingredients in the order listed. Spread batter in an ungreased 13"x9" baking pan. Bake at 350 degrees for 25 to 30 minutes, until center is set. Let cool and cut into squares. Makes 20.

93

Nikki Matusiak
Zelienople, PA

These have replaced the usual variety as our family's favorite brownie...delicious!

Baby Rattle Cupcakes

18-1/2 oz. pkg. yellow cake mix
16-oz. container white frosting
red and blue food colorings
24 lollipops, unwrapped
Garnish: large candy sprinkles
Optional: bows

Follow the package instructions to prepare cake mix and bake in paper-lined muffin cups; let cool. Spoon Vanilla Glaze over cupcakes; let stand until set, about 10 minutes. Divide frosting in half; use a few drops of food coloring to tint one half pink and the other half blue. Place each colored frosting in a plastic zipping bag; snip off a tip and pipe designs onto cupcakes. Attach candy sprinkles with a dot of frosting. Insert a lollipop in the side of each cupcake; tie on bows, if desired. Makes 2 dozen.

Vanilla Glaze:

3 c. powdered sugar
3 T. water
2 T. light corn syrup
1/2 t. vanilla extract

Beat all ingredients until smooth.

Tori Willis
Champaign, IL
You can tint the frosting to match Baby's nursery...
so sweet!

Birthday Cake Cookies

16-1/2 oz. tube refrigerated sugar
    cookie dough
16-oz. container white frosting
few drops desired food coloring
Garnish: candy sprinkles
10 birthday candles

Shape 1/3 of cookie dough into 10, one-inch balls; press into bottoms and up sides of lightly greased mini muffin cups. Shape remaining dough into 10 equal balls; press into bottoms and up sides of lightly greased regular muffin cups. Bake at 350 degrees; bake mini cookies 8 to 9 minutes; bake regular cookies 10 to 11 minutes. Cool 5 minutes in tins on wire racks. Remove cookies to wire racks; cool completely. Tint the frosting with food coloring. Spread frosting over top and sides of each cookie. Place one mini cookie on top of one regular cookie. Decorate with sprinkles. Press a candle into center of each cookie. Makes 10.

95

Nancy Wise
Little Rock, AR

I'm the baker in the family and my granddaughter, Hannah, isn't fond of cake. I made these for her eighth birthday and she was tickled pink!

Be Mine Cherry Brownies

Dana Cunningham
Lafayette, LA
Bake an extra-special Valentine for your sweetie!

18.3-oz. pkg. fudge brownie mix
3 1-oz. sqs. white baking chocolate
1/3 c. whipping cream
1 c. cream cheese frosting
1/4 c. maraschino cherries,
    drained and chopped
1-1/2 c. semi-sweet chocolate chips
1/4 c. butter
Garnish: candy sprinkles

Prepare brownie mix according to package instructions. Line a 13"x9" baking pan with aluminum foil, leaving several inches on sides for handles. Spray bottom of foil with non-stick vegetable spray; spread batter into pan. Bake at 350 degrees for 24 to 26 minutes; let cool. Lift brownies from pan; remove foil. Use a 3-inch heart-shaped cookie cutter to cut brownies. In a microwave-safe bowl, melt white baking chocolate and whipping cream for one to 2 minutes, stirring until chocolate is melted; refrigerate 30 minutes. Stir frosting and cherries into chilled chocolate mixture; spread over brownies. In a microwave-safe bowl, melt chocolate chips and butter for one to 2 minutes, stirring until smooth. Transfer to a plastic zipping bag, snip off a tip and drizzle over brownies. Garnish with sprinkles. Makes 14.

Emerald Isle Cupcakes

1-3/4 c. all-purpose flour
2/3 c. sugar
3.4-oz. pkg. instant pistachio
  pudding mix
1-1/2 t. baking powder
1/2 t. salt
2 eggs, beaten
1-1/4 c. milk
1/2 c. oil
1/2 t. vanilla extract
few drops green food coloring
16-oz. container cream cheese
  frosting
Garnish: candy sprinkles

In a bowl, combine flour, sugar,
dry pudding mix, baking powder
and salt. In another bowl, beat eggs,
milk, oil and vanilla; add to flour
mixture and mix until well blended.
Fill paper-lined muffin cups 2/3 full.
Bake at 375 degrees for 20 to
25 minutes, until a toothpick tests
clean. Cool in tin on a wire rack. Add
a few drops of food coloring to the
frosting and frost the cupcakes.
Garnish with sprinkles. Makes
1-1/2 dozen.

Jackie Smulski
Lyons, IL
These cupcakes are not
only good for St. Patrick's
Day but are a refreshing
treat to welcome the
first day of spring.

Easter Ice Cream Sandwiches

17-1/2 oz. pkg. sugar cookie mix
assorted food colorings
1 pt. vanilla ice cream, softened
Optional: 2 c. sweetened flaked
   coconut

Prepare cookie dough following package instructions. Reserve one cup of dough. Roll out remaining dough on a floured surface 1/4-inch thick. Use a 3-inch egg-shaped cookie cutter to cut dough. Divide reserved dough in thirds; tint with food coloring as desired. Form colored dough into small balls and ropes and arrange on half the cookies. Place on ungreased baking sheets. Bake at 350 degrees for 7 to 9 minutes. Cool on baking sheets one minute; remove cookies to cool completely on wire rack. Position plain cookie on bottom, spread with ice cream and top with decorated cookie. Gently press together; freeze until serving time. If desired, mix a few drops of green food coloring and coconut; let dry on wax paper. Fill a platter or ramekins with coconut. Arrange sandwiches on top. Makes about one dozen.

Anna McMaster
Portland, OR

Wrap these springtime treats in pastel-colored plastic wrap and store in the freezer until ready to serve.

Flowerpot Cupcakes

Joanna Nicoline-Haughey
Berwyn, PA

These pretty cupcakes
are perfect for
Mothers' Day!

18-1/2 oz. pkg. favorite-flavor
    cake mix
20 flat-bottomed ice cream cones
16-oz. container favorite-flavor
    frosting
Garnish: candy sprinkles
20 lollipops, unwrapped
20 spearmint candy leaves

Prepare cake mix as directed on
package. Fill ice cream cones
3/4 full. Arrange on ungreased
baking sheets or in muffin tins. Bake
at 350 degrees for 18 to 20 minutes.
Let cool completely. Frost cupcakes
and garnish with sprinkles. Insert a
lollipop into the center of each
cupcake. Arrange candy leaves on
frosting at the base of the lollipop
stick. Makes 20.

99

Bride & Groom Cookies

Nola Coons
Gooseberry Patch

I made these for my niece's bridal shower...she was thrilled! You'll find meringue powder and black gel paste food coloring at craft stores.

17-1/2 oz. pkg. sugar cookie mix
Royal Icing (recipe on page 106)

Following package instructions, prepare and bake sugar cookies using a 2-inch heart-shaped cookie cutter; let cool. Spoon one cup each of the Royal Icing and Black Royal icing into separate plastic zipping bags. Seal bags and snip off a tip on each. Referring to photo, pipe outlines of white Royal Icing and Black Royal Icing onto the cookies. Let icing set. Thin remaining icings with a little water and use a spoon to spread the icing on the cookies, filling in the outlines. Makes 2 dozen.

Black Royal Icing:

2 c. powdered sugar
2-1/2 T. baking cocoa
1-1/2 T. meringue powder
black gel paste food coloring
2 to 4 T. warm water

Use an electric mixer to combine powdered sugar, cocoa and meringue powder. Mix in gel paste coloring until desired color. Gradually beat in water until icing is desired consistency. Beat on medium-high speed until glossy, 5 to 7 minutes.

Dad's Giant Cookie

2-1/4 c. all-purpose flour
1 t. baking powder
1/2 t. salt
1 c. butter, softened
1-1/2 c. brown sugar, packed
1 t. vanilla extract
2 eggs
2 c. milk chocolate chips
16-oz. container chocolate
    frosting
7-oz. tube blue decorator icing
Garnish: milk chocolate chunks,
    mini marshmallows, peanuts

In a small bowl, combine flour, baking powder and salt; set aside. Use an electric mixer on medium speed to beat together butter, brown sugar and vanilla for 5 minutes. Add eggs, one at a time, beating well after each addition. Gradually beat in flour mixture; stir in chocolate chips. Spread batter on a 14" round pizza pan lined with parchment paper. Bake at 375 degrees for 30 to 40 minutes, until golden. Cool in pan for 10 minutes. Transfer to a serving platter to cool completely. Decorate as desired with chocolate frosting and blue icing. Sprinkle edges with garnishes as desired. To serve, cut into wedges. Serves 12.

Elizabeth Blackstone
Racine, WI

What better way to celebrate a big-hearted dad than with a big, hearty cookie?

IOI

Fourth of July Lemon Bars

16-1/2 oz. pkg. lemon bar mix
1/4 c. powdered sugar
.68-oz. tube red decorating gel
1/4 c. blueberries

Prepare lemon bars as directed on package; bake in an ungreased 9"x9" baking pan. Cool completely in pan on a wire rack. Cut into 6 rectangular bars. Place bars on a serving plate. Sprinkle with powdered sugar. Pipe stripes across bars with decorating gel. Place 6 blueberries in the top corner of each bar. Makes 6.

Marlene Darnell
Newport Beach, CA

With a few simple decorations, your dessert will be the hit of the picnic!

Scaredy-Cat Cookies

1 c. butter, softened
2 c. sugar
2 eggs, beaten
1 T. vanilla extract
3 c. all-purpose flour
1 c. baking cocoa
1/2 t. baking powder
1/2 t. baking soda
1/2 t. salt
48 pieces candy corn
24 red cinnamon candies

In a bowl, combine butter and sugar. Beat in eggs and vanilla. In a separate bowl, combine flour, cocoa, baking powder, baking soda and salt; gradually add to butter mixture. Roll dough into 1-1/2 inch balls. Place 3 inches apart on lightly greased baking sheets. Flatten with a glass dipped in sugar. Pinch tops of cookie to form ears. For whiskers, press a fork twice into each cookie. Bake at 350 degrees for 7 to 8 minutes, until almost set. Remove from oven; immediately press on candy corn for eyes and cinnamon candies for noses. Remove to wire racks to cool. Makes 2 dozen.

Kay Marone
Des Moines, IA
Kids love to make and eat these cute Halloween goodies!

103

Spooky Skull Cupcakes

18-1/2 oz. pkg. white cake mix
12 marshmallows
16-oz. can vanilla frosting
Garnish: mini chocolate-covered
    mints, chocolate chips,
    slivered almonds

Prepare cake mix as package directs;
bake in 24 paper-lined muffin cups.
Cool. Cut each marshmallow in half
from top to bottom. Carefully pull each
paper liner partially away from
cupcake; tuck a marshmallow half
between liner and cupcake to create jaw
of skull. Spread frosting over cupcake
and marshmallow. Add mints dotted
with white frosting for eyes, a chocolate
chip for a nose and slivered almonds
for teeth. Makes 2 dozen.

John Alexander
New Britain, CT
Get really scary and use
cinnamon candies for
the eyes...yikes!

Tom Turkey Cupcakes

18-1/2 oz. pkg. yellow cake mix
16-oz. container chocolate
  frosting
1/2 c. white frosting
2 11-oz. pkgs. candy corn
Garnish: chocolate sprinkles

Follow the package instructions to prepare cake mix and bake in 24 paper-lined muffin cups. Let cool completely. Frost each cupcake completely with chocolate icing. Spoon or pipe a dollop of icing for the head. Put 5 pieces of candy corn along the back side for the feathers. Place one candy corn on the front of the cupcake for the beak. Sprinkle chocolate sprinkles over the chocolate icing, about halfway. Pipe the eyes above the beak with white frosting. Place a sprinkle in the center of each eye. Makes 2 dozen.

Amy Jones
Graham, NC
I just baked these this year and hope to continue the tradition with my son each Thanksgiving as a special memory.

"Oh, Christmas Tree" Cookies

17-1/2 oz. pkg. sugar cookie mix
several drops green food coloring
Garnish: assorted candy sprinkles

Prepare cookie dough according to
package directions; mix in food
coloring. Cover and refrigerate
3 hours. On a lightly floured surface,
roll dough to 1/4-inch thickness. Cut
dough with a 3-inch tree-shaped cookie
cutter. Place on ungreased baking
sheets. Bake at 350 degrees for 7 to
9 minutes. Immediately cut half the
cookies in half vertically; trim bottom
of all tree trunks so they are straight.
Cool on baking sheets one minute; cool
completely on wire racks. Color half
the Royal Icing with green food
coloring. Spread green icing down cut
edge of a half cookie. Press a half cookie
to center of a whole cookie; let set.
Attach a half cookie to back of the
whole cookie. Decorate as desired.
Makes about 2 dozen.

Royal Icing:

2 c. powdered sugar
1-1/2 T. meringue powder
2 to 4 T. warm water

Combine powdered sugar and
meringue powder. With an electric
mixer, gradually beat in water until
icing is desired consistency. Beat until
glossy, 5 to 7 minutes.

Sarah Oravecz
Gooseberry Patch

These three-dimensional
cookies can be adapted to
any holiday. Just use your
favorite cookie cutter and
trim the cookie bottoms so
they're straight...how fun!

Frosty the Cupcake

8-1/2 oz. pkg. favorite-flavor
    cake mix
1/2 c. creamy peanut butter
24 round buttery crackers
2 6-oz. pkgs. white baking
    chocolate, coarsely chopped
1 c. mini semi-sweet chocolate
    chips
12 pieces candy corn, yellow
    ends removed
24 pieces red candy-coated
    chocolates
.68-oz. tube red decorating gel
16-oz. container white frosting
Garnish: blue candy sprinkles

107

Follow the package directions to
prepare cake mix and bake in paper-
lined muffin cups; let cool. Spread
peanut butter over half the crackers;
top with remaining crackers. In a
microwave-safe bowl, melt white
chocolate for one to 2 minutes; stir
until smooth. Dip each sandwich in
chocolate and let excess drip off; set
on wax paper. Immediately place
chocolate chips for eyes and mouth
and candy corn for nose. Place a
candy-coated chocolate on each side
of the face and connect with a line of
red decorating gel. Let set. Frost
cupcakes with frosting and garnish
with sprinkles. Top with a snowman
sandwich. Makes one dozen.

Jo Ann
Almost too cute to eat!
Double this recipe for
your holiday open house.

INDEX

INDEX

Bears at the Beach, page 17

Buttermilk Sugar Cookies, page 53

Cream Cheese Crescent Bars, page 69

Thanks, Mom!

Flowerpot Cupcakes, page 99

Our Story

Back in 1984, we were next-door neighbors raising our families in the little town of Delaware, Ohio. We were two moms with small children looking for a way to do what we loved and stay home with the kids too. We shared a love of home cooking and making memories with family & friends. After many a conversation over the backyard fence, **Gooseberry Patch** was born.

We put together the first catalog & cookbooks at our kitchen tables and packed boxes from the basement, enlisting the help of our loved ones wherever we could. From that little family, we've grown to include an amazing group of creative folks who love cooking, decorating and creating as much as we do.

Hard to believe it's been over 25 years since those kitchen-table days. Today we're best known for our homestyle, family-friendly cookbooks, now recognized as national bestsellers! We love hand-picking the recipes and are tickled to share our inspiration, ideas and more with you. One thing's for sure, we couldn't have done it without our friends all across the country. Whether you've been along for the ride from the beginning or are just discovering us, welcome to our family!

Vickie & Jo Ann

1·800·854·6673

Visit us online:

www.gooseberrypatch.com

U.S. to Canadian Recipe Equivalents

Volume Measurements

1/4 teaspoon	1 mL
1/2 teaspoon	2 mL
1 teaspoon	5 mL
1 tablespoon = 3 teaspoons	15 mL
2 tablespoons = 1 fluid ounce	30 mL
1/4 cup	60 mL
1/3 cup	75 mL
1/2 cup = 4 fluid ounces	125 mL
1 cup = 8 fluid ounces	250 mL
2 cups = 1 pint =16 fluid ounces	500 mL
4 cups = 1 quart	1 L

Weights

1 ounce	30 g
4 ounces	120 g
8 ounces	225 g
16 ounces = 1 pound	450 g

Oven Temperatures

300° F	150° C
325° F	160° C
350° F	180° C
375° F	190° C
400° F	200° C
450° F	230° C

Baking Pan Sizes

Square

8x8x2 inches	2 L = 20x20x5 cm
9x9x2 inches	2.5 L = 23x23x5 cm

Rectangular

13x9x2 inches	3.5 L = 33x23x5 cm

Loaf

9x5x3 inches	2 L = 23x13x7 cm

Round

8x1-1/2 inches	1.2 L = 20x4 cm
9x1-1/2 inches	1.5 L = 23x4 cm

Recipe Abbreviations

t. = teaspoon	ltr. = liter
T. = tablespoon	oz. = ounce
c. = cup	lb. = pound
pt. = pint	doz. = dozen
qt. = quart	pkg. = package
gal. = gallon	env. = envelope

Kitchen Measurements

A pinch = 1/8 tablespoon	1 fluid ounce = 2 tablespoons
3 teaspoons = 1 tablespoon	4 fluid ounces = 1/2 cup
2 tablespoons = 1/8 cup	8 fluid ounces = 1 cup
4 tablespoons = 1/4 cup	16 fluid ounces = 1 pint
8 tablespoons = 1/2 cup	32 fluid ounces = 1 quart
16 tablespoons = 1 cup	16 ounces net weight = 1 pound
2 cups = 1 pint	
4 cups = 1 quart	
4 quarts = 1 gallon	